SPECTRUM®
READERS

MW00948643

PROTECT!

Wild Animals

By Teresa Domnauer

Carson-Dellosa
Publishing

An imprint of Carson-Dellosa Publishing, LLC
P.O. Box 35665
Greensboro, NC 27425-5665

carsondellosa.com

Printed in the USA. All rights reserved.
ISBN 978-1-4838-0122-3

01-002141120

We share the planet with animals.
They need food, water, and shelter,
just like humans do.
Hunting, clearing trees, and building
roads can make it hard for some animals
to survive.
But, there is hope for threatened and
endangered animals.
People are working hard to help them.

Black Rhino

Black rhinos need our protection.
Hunters kill rhinos for their horns.
By 1995, only 2,400 wild black rhinos
were left.
African countries joined together to
protect them.
Today, their population has nearly
doubled in size.

Red Wolf

Red wolves need our protection.
These shy animals once roamed the
eastern United States.
They were hunted almost to extinction.
A protection and breeding program is
underway for these animals.
Now, over 100 wild red wolves live in
North Carolina.

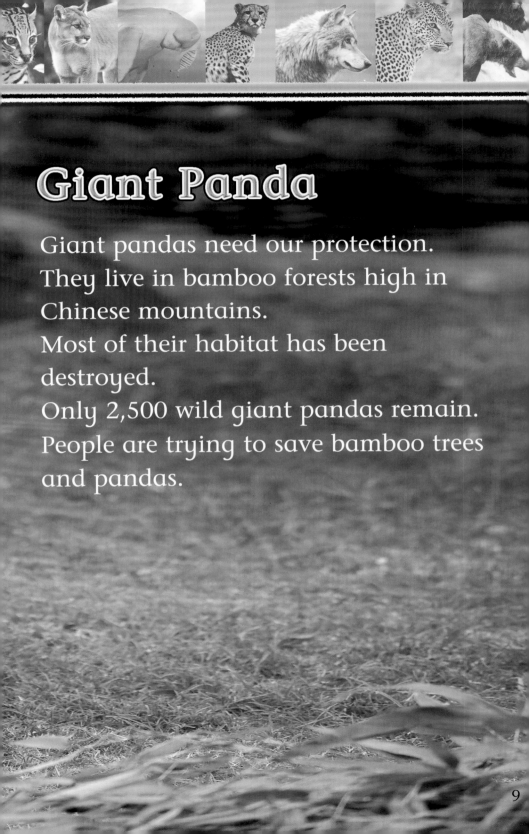

Giant Panda

Giant pandas need our protection.
They live in bamboo forests high in
Chinese mountains.
Most of their habitat has been
destroyed.
Only 2,500 wild giant pandas remain.
People are trying to save bamboo trees
and pandas.

Siberian Tiger

Siberian tigers need our protection.
Just 400 wild Siberian tigers remain.
They live in cold parts of Asia.
Scientists put radio collars on some of
these tigers.
Radio signals reveal how the tigers
live and breed.
Better understanding will help people
protect tigers.

Chimpanzee

Chimpanzees need our protection. They are threatened when people live too close to them. Chimps can catch human diseases. Chimpanzee groups are stranded when forests are cut down. People are planting trees to help connect chimpanzee groups.

Jaguar

Jaguars need our protection.
People thought they were extinct in the
United States.
Then, a few jaguars were spotted in
Arizona and New Mexico.
They may have traveled from Mexico.
Now, special laws protect jaguars in
these states.

American Bison

American bison need our protection.
Millions of bison once covered the
grasslands of the United States.
In the 19th century, hunters nearly
eliminated them.
Today, herds of wild bison live at
Yellowstone National Park.

Ocelot

Ocelots need our protection.
People hunt them illegally for their beautiful, patterned skins.
Only about 100 wild ocelots are left in Texas.
People have a plan to bring ocelots from Mexico to Texas for breeding.

Cougar

Cougars need our protection.
People sometimes kill them for preying on farm animals.
Scientists are learning that cougars are important for the environment.
They help control the deer population.
New laws protect these big cats.

Dugong

Dugongs need our protection.
They get tangled in fishing nets and hit by boats.
These gentle sea mammals live off the coast of Australia.
Conservation groups are teaching others how to protect dugongs and their ocean habitats.

Cheetah

Cheetahs need our protection.
African farmers kill cheetahs that hunt
their livestock.
A conservation group has a solution.
It brings Anatolian guard dogs to farms.
The trained dogs protect farm animals,
and cheetahs stay safe.

Gray Wolf

Gray wolves need our protection.
They were once the most widespread
mammals in the world.
Today, they are endangered in many
places.
In the 1990s, wolves were released in
Yellowstone National Park.
They have improved the park's
ecosystem.

28

Leopard

Leopards need our protection.
African farmers kill leopards that prey on livestock.
Conservation groups put bomas on farmland to help leopards.
Bomas are predator-proof enclosures.
They protect farm animals and leopards.

Grizzly Bear

Grizzly bears need our protection. Outside Alaska, only about 1,500 wild grizzly bears live in the U.S. The bears need room to roam, but roads and buildings block them. People design and build tunnels to let grizzlies pass under roads.

PROTECT! Wild Animals Comprehension Questions

1. Name three human activities that threaten animal survival.

2. Where do most dugongs live?

3. When were wolves released in Yellowstone National Park?

4. Where do giant pandas live?

5. Why is it dangerous for chimpanzees to live near humans?

6. Why are ocelots hunted?

7. How do cougars help the environment?

8. What is a boma?

9. How can livestock-protecting dogs help cheetahs?

10. How many grizzly bears are left in the